LESLEY ANNE IVORY'S

CHRISTMAS CATS

CRESCENT
BOOKS
New York • Avenel

INTRODUCTION

*H*appy are the Christmases that are shared with cats! There is no doubt in my mind about cats being aware of Christmas. They are certainly responsive to atmospheres, and are receptive to the gathering activity of the human family in its preparations for Christmas. They enjoy, watch and anticipate the goodwill and generous feelings that abound at this festive time. They love all the intriguing rattlings of paper, the pretty strings and wonderful cooking smells coming from the kitchen, and watching the glint of Christmas decorations on the pine-scented tree lit by the flicker of firelight.

My cats really love Christmas and I have seen them pondering with extra thoughtfulness through the window as if waiting for something to happen. Everyone who shares Christmas with cats is especially enriched, and it is this mutual delight that I have attempted to express in my paintings.

Lesley Anne Ivory

GEMMA AND THE PINK
SUGAR MOUSE

'Twas the night before Christmas,
when all through the house
Not a creature was stirring,
not even a mouse;

Clement Clarke Moore, *A Visit from St Nicholas*

*G*emma, my silver-spotted tabby and white, really prefers other sorts of mice to these sugar ones, but it is Christmas and she finds it quite interesting that one has mysteriously moved from the border – the sort of magic that happens only at Christmas.

MANUEL IN THE
CHRISTMAS ROBIN BAG

The robin seems to be fond of the com-
pany and haunts of man ... we had
one that used to come in at a broken
pane in the window three winters
together. It grew so tame that it would
perch on one's finger and take the
crumbs out of the hand. It was much
startled at the cat at first, but after a
time it took little notice of her further
than always contriving to keep out of
her way.

John Clare, *The Robin*

*M*anuel, who is Agneatha's kitten,
loves robins at any time of the
year, and has the sort of innocence in
his expression that assures us that little
Christmas robins could not possibly ever
melt in his mouth.

BLOSSOM UNDER THE MISTLETOE

Sitting under the mistletoe
(Pale green, fairy mistletoe)
One last candle burning low,
All the sleepy dancers gone,
Just one candle burning on,
Shadows lurking everywhere:
Someone came, and kissed me there.

Walter de la Mare, *Mistletoe*

*B*lossom is waiting hopefully under the mistletoe, with lights that came from my parents' house. She has breathed through the frosty window to see her friend opposite. Blossom has eccentric tastes – she loves garlic, for example – but Christmas is her special time of the year as she also adores mince pies.

OCTOPUSSY WITH CHRISTMAS DECORATIONS

The singing waits, a merry throng,
At early morn, with simple skill,
Yet imitate the angel's song,
And chant their Christmas ditty still;
And, mid the storm that dies and swells
By fits, in hummings softly steals
The music of the village bells,
Ringing round their merry peals.

John Clare, *December*

*O*ctopussy is very interested in sorting out my Christmas decorations, some of which are over fifty years old. The delicate little green glass horn can still be blown. Octopussy has been a part of my Christmases for the past eight years – which is appropriate for the eighth kitten born on the eighth day of the eighth month.

AGNEATHA WITH THE APPLE

When they were all tired of blind-
man's buff, there was a great game at
snapdragon, and when fingers enough
were burned with that, and all the
raisins gone, they sat down by the
huge fire of blazing logs to a sub-
stantial supper, and a mighty bowl of
wassail, something smaller than an
ordinary washhouse copper, in which
the hot apples were hissing and bub-
bling with a rich look, and a jolly
sound, that were perfectly irresistible.
"This," said Mr Pickwick, looking
round him, "this is, indeed, comfort."

Charles Dickens, *Pickwick Papers*

The night of Christmas Eve, and
Agneatha is serenely contemplating
Christmas, tuned in to her own feline
Christmas wavelength. I designed the
wallpaper around her to illustrate one of
my favourite carols, *The Holly and the
Ivy*, and a little robin is woven amongst
the greenery.

MAU-MAU AND
THE CHRISTMAS CARD

I myself think much of Christmas and all its associations ... I like the festoons of holly on the walls and windows; the dance under the mistletoe; the gigantic sausage; the baron of beef; the vast globe of plum-pudding, the true image of the earth, flattened at the poles; the tapping of the old October; the inexhaustible bowl of punch; the life and joy of the old hall, when the squire and his household and his neighbourhood were as one.

Thomas Love Peacock, *Gryll Grange*

Mau-Mau has heard the postman dropping more Christmas cards through the letterbox. Christmas cards have always fascinated her. She is sure that this little blue cat card has been sent for her. The window is in a neighbour's house, and to draw it for this picture I sat on the stairs, squeezed between their two watching children, the dog and three cats.

SPIRO'S CHRISTMAS
STOCKING

Brilliantly vivid, the morning of my
last nursery Christmas returns to me.
Waking at a preposterously early hour,
I shook Colin out of his deep sleep to
share the thrill of the first tentative
probings of the bulges in our heavily
weighted stockings, before, full of wild
surmise, we dragged out the rustling
parcels, and fumbled with knotted
string and crackling paper until our
cots were heaped high with the litter
of unpacking.

Cynthia Asquith, *Haply I May Remember*

Christmas Eve, and Spiro is keeping a
Christmas stocking warm, and waiting to see what might happen, purring a
private cat carol to himself, and hoping
that on Christmas Day he will wake up
to find it full of fresh pink prawns, his
favourite treat. The Indian patterned
carpet is from my parents' house where
I was born. The colours in it suit Spiro's
soft ginger fur.

RUSKIN IN THE
CHRISTMAS NIGHT WINDOW

Stately, kindly, lordly friend,
Condescend
Here to sit by me, and turn
Glorious eyes that smile and burn,
Golden eyes, love's lustrous meed,
On the golden page I read.

Algernon Swinburne, *To a Cat*

*T*he floodlit old church in Hitchin, Hertfordshire, and its Christmas trees form the glowing background for Ruskin's Christmas portrait. He is probably imagining that he can hear sleigh bells in the indigo velvet sky. He is the most nostalgic and thoughtful cat, and Christmas gives food for thought to his feline imaginings – or is it the smell of festive fare coming from the kitchen that rivets his attention so?

CHRISTIE LOOKING FOR
FATHER CHRISTMAS

Be merry all,
Be merry all,
With holly dress the festive hall;
Prepare the song, the feast, the ball,
To welcome merry Christmas.

William Robert Spencer

Christie, who is our son Julian's cat, is gazing up at the snowy Christmas sky through his country cottage window with great wonderment and anticipation. Even a little kitten understands what an exciting and special time it is for everyone. Soon afterwards, when Julian was out, she and her brother and sister who live with her re-wove the lace curtains during a boisterously festive romp.

HARRY AND SHEENA AND
THE CHRISTMAS PRESENTS

Time was with most of us, when
Christmas Day, encircling all our
limited world like a magic ring, left
nothing out for us to miss or seek;
bound together all our home enjoy-
ments, affections and hopes; grouped
every thing and every one round the
Christmas fire, and made the little
picture shining in our bright young
eyes, complete.

Charles Dickens,
What Christmas Is, As We Grow Older

*J*ames's young cats Harry and Sheena
get into everything – including the
presents. They examine all the parcels,
sniffing and patting them to see if they
move, and wonder which ones are for
them. Our cats always have presents,
which range from small tins of salmon
to herb-stuffed toys. They give us presents too – unwrapped and not always
acceptable, among them stolen goods
and assorted small wildlife – left on the
doorstep for us to find.

SHEENA AND THE LANTERNS

The walls and ceiling were so hung
with living green that it looked a perfect grove, from every part of which
bright gleaming berries glistened. The
crisp leaves of holly, mistletoe and ivy
reflected back the light, as if so many
little mirrors had been scattered there.

Charles Dickens, *A Christmas Carol*

My father bought me these
Christmas tree lanterns when I
was five. They have graced our annual
tree ever since. This year their glow
falls on Sheena, who is celebrating her
first Christmas. My grandfather grew
Chinese lanterns in his garden, and at
Christmas time, many years ago, Granny
used to arrange them in the same vase
that is now behind Sheena.

AGNEATHA AND HER CHRISTMAS DECORATION

She struck another match, and suddenly she was sitting under the most beautiful Christmas tree. A thousand candles lit up the green branches, and gaily coloured balls like those in the shop windows looked down upon her. The many candles on the Christmas tree rose higher and higher through the air, and she saw that they had now turned into bright stars.

Hans Christian Andersen, *The Little Match Girl*

*A*gneatha has her back to the cityscape of St Albans, shining with its Christmas illuminations. She stares into the warm room and watches her family enjoying Christmas. A tree ball has been created with her portrait on it, of which she is very proud. This ball – and her beauty – were my inspiration for this Christmas design.

OCTOPUSSY AND HIS
CHRISTMAS DECORATION

The hall was full of children, and
there, on the dais, in isolated splen-
dour, stood the great tree, shining
with a hundred candles and glittering
with a hundred baubles of coloured
glass . . . a spangled doll, a fairy queen
with a crescent in her hair, gloriously
crowned the topmost spike. Toys were
heaped upon the table; a hamper of
oranges and a hamper of rosy apples
stood ready on either side, the lids
thrown back.

Vita Sackville-West, *The Edwardians*

*L*ike Agneatha, his mother, Octopussy
has had a Christmas tree decoration
created featuring himself in the design,
and the little wooden box beside him
matches it. He would rather chase the
ball around, but he is allowed only to
look at it and admire his reflection, and
to watch the firelight flickering in the
little stars.

MOTLEY AND THE
CHRISTMAS PUDDINGS

At one end of the hall was a group of the young folks, some nearly grown up, others of a more tender and budding age, fully engrossed by a merry game; and a profusion of wooden horses, penny trumpets, and tattered dolls, about the floor, showed traces of little fairy beings, who having frolicked through a happy day had been carried off to slumber through a peaceful night.

Washington Irving, *Old Christmas*

*A*fter the presents have been unwrapped and the brightly patterned papers and ribbons lie in abandoned profusion all around her, Motley is found warmly nestling in their midst, feeling most Christdingly*, and settling her Christmas dinner. A perfect ending to a happy Christmas Day.

*A local word, much used in the Ivory household,
evoking the tingle we sense at Christmas.

With love to Peggy and Tony (who love Christmas so much)

My cats wish all cats, everywhere, as warm
and happy a Christmas as theirs.

This 1996 edition is published by Crescent Books,
a division of Random House Value Publishing, Inc.,
40 Engelhard Avenue, Avenel, New Jersey 07001.

Crescent Books and colophon are trademarks of
Random House Value Publishing, Inc.

Random House
New York • Toronto • London • Sydney • Auckland

Manufactured in Hong Kong

A CIP catalog record for this book is available
from the Library of Congress.

ISBN 0-517-16021-8

8 7 6 5 4 3 2 1